PATISSERIE

& CONFECTIONERY

N V Q / S V Q   L E V E L   3   W O R K B O O K

PATISSERIE & CONFECTIONERY

NVQ/SVQ LEVEL 3 WORKBOOK

To be used in conjunction with *Advanced Practical Cookery*
and also *The Theory of Catering* and *Practical Cookery*

Victor Ceserani, Ronald Kinton and David Foskett
with additional questions by John Huber

Hodder & Stoughton
A MEMBER OF THE HODDER HEADLINE GROUP

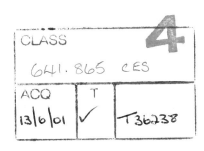
British Library Cataloguing in Publication Data
Ceserani, Victor
   Pâtisserie and confectionery. – (NVQ/SVQ workbook. Level 3)
   1. Caterers and catering   2. Food service   3. Confectionery
   I. Title   II. Kinton, Ronald   III. Foskett, David, 1951–
   642.5

ISBN 0 340 67389 3

First published 1996
Impression number 10 9 8 7 6 5 4 3 2 1
Year   2000 1999 1998 1997 1996

Typeset by Wearset, Boldon, Tyne and Wear.
Printed in Great Britain for Hodder & Stoughton Educational, a division of Hodder Headline Plc, 338 Euston Road, London NW1 3BH by the Bath Press.

Contents

Introduction

The aim of this book is to develop the candidate's underpinning knowledge in order to carry out the competence required to achieve NVQ/SVQ level 3 in Pâtisserie and Confectionery. It is intended solely for the candidate's own use and self-assessment.

In addition to learning the skills of food preparation and cooking, it is necessary to develop an inquiring mind, a knowledge of the commodities used and the reasons why practical work is carried out in certain ways. In other words, the theory of food and cooking.

The purpose of this workbook is to assist students in developing a systematic approach to combining theory with practice, which is essential for a proper understanding of the skills involved.

Candidates are advised to develop an attitude of mind so that, whenever working in practical situations, they are always thinking *why* the various processes are used and *about* the commodities. Similarly, when working through this book, they should be thinking of the practical situation in relation to the theory.

Never separate theory and practice in the mind – the two should at all times complement each other to develop a helpful, deeper understanding.

National and Scottish Vocational Qualifications (NVQ/SVQ)

A National or Scottish Vocational Qualification is awarded following a method of assessment to candidates achieving the required level of ability. These levels are:

- level 1: Operative
- level 2: Craft
- level 3: Supervisory
- level 4: Junior management

Assessment occurs at work, and/or college in a realistic working environment and is available to all irrespective of age and entry qualification requirements. The system enables the participants to progress through the levels in a flexible manner according to individual circumstances and abilities. Previous experience and knowledge are taken into account.

Candidates are fully involved in the assessment procedure by the completion of an evidence diary recording their performance. This provides evidence of activities carried out in a working environment while being assessed.

Understanding, underpinning knowledge or related theory is assessed orally or by the use of visual or other aids and, for levels 3/4, written questions may be used.

Recording assessment details

With all aspects of dealing with training, people's records must always be stored securely and available only to those authorised to have access to them.

- Past records should be valid, accurate relevant and reliable.
- Current information about learners must also be valid, accurate relevant and reliable.
- All interpretation of records must be fair and justified.

The records should be kept together and form the portfolio of evidence and may include audio and video tapes.

It is essential at the outset that all records are retained and may include:

- completed record units;
- assessment plans;
- oral/written questions used during assessment;
- any case studies or role plays used;
- work-based projects;
- accreditation of prior learning assessment plans;
- details of accreditation of prior learning advised or assessed;
- references and letters of validation;
- records of meeting with assessors and verifiers;
- certificates;
- documented feedback given to candidates.

A candidate needs to ensure that the contents of his/her portfolio are relevant to the performance criteria and range of elements being worked towards.

This book is a sister volume to *NVQ/SVQ Workbook Level 3, Kitchen and Larder Work* (1996), and comprises half of *NVQ/SVQ Level 3 Food Preparation and Cookery* (1995); all are written by the same team of authors, and are published by Hodder & Stoughton.

MANAGING RESOURCES AND
THE ENVIRONMENT

Unit 3B2

Control the receipt, storage and issue of resources

Read *Advanced Practical Cookery* pages 6–11.

<u>3B2.1</u> *Monitor and control the receipt of goods*

The receiving area is prepared and staff are available to take receipt of deliveries.

1   Who would take receipt of deliveries?

    ....

2   What preparation is required prior to delivery of goods?

    ....

Goods received are matched against documented information and discrepancies are identified.

3   What documents are needed on receipt of goods?

    ....

4   What do you understand by 'discrepancies'?

    ....

Goods are matched against purchasing specifications and deviations are identified.

5   What is a purchasing specification?

    ....

6   Give examples of specifications for raspberries and racks of lamb.

    ....

    ....

    ....

7 What deviations may occur when, for example, raspberries are delivered?

....

Discrepancies and deviations are investigated thoroughly and prompt action is taken to rectify any problems and minimise disruption to operations.

8 What prompt action should be taken?

....

9 Give an example of a typical problem.

....

10 How may disruption be minimised?

....

Goods are transported to the appropriate storage area within the necessary timescale and in accordance with relevant legislation.

11 State why goods on delivery should be quickly taken to the correct storage area.

....

12 What precautions should be taken with:

Frozen foods? ....

Fresh fish? ....

13 What happens to refrigerated storage if the doors are open for a long period of time?

....

Security procedures are fully maintained.

14 Who is responsible for the security of goods?

....

15   What procedures would be taken in an organisation to prevent the stealing of goods?

....

16   Does a system of documentation help to prevent pilfering? If so, explain how.

....

17   What should you do if you become aware that items are disappearing?
   Report it to your immediate superior?
   Call the police?
   Do nothing?
   Check the organisation's policy in such matters?

3B2.2   *Control the storage of stocks/goods*

The storage of perishable items, non-perishable items and hazardous items in any establishment must be thorough. Legal requirements must be complied with regarding safety and hygiene. Goods must be secure to prevent stealing and an effective system of control to prevent wastage, over-ordering and under-ordering should be in force.

Items of a hazardous nature must be kept secure. This applies particularly to certain cleaning items, for example, bleach, ammonia, disinfectants and oven cleaners.

Checks on all items are essential. These may be spot checks taken at random for particular items to see that records are accurate, as well as a full stock audit to check all the goods in store. The information obtained identifies losses and deterioration, as well as inappropriate ordering. Having too much of an item is not practising economy effectively; however, purchasing in bulk may be economical provided storage space is not a problem.

Storage facilities are fully prepared and maintained under the correct conditions.

1   For correct storage conditions other than hygiene, give two examples and explain why you have stated them.

....

....

2   Explain what you understand by storage facilities being properly maintained.

....

....

3   Name four non-food items and state where they should be stored.

   ....

   ....

   ....

   ....

4   Name two hazardous items and state how they should be stored.

   ....

   ....

5   Explain what you understand by stock rotation and state why it is necessary.

   ....

6   What policy has your organisation implemented regarding stock rotation?

   ....

Stock is stored and handled in accordance with product instructions, organisational policy and relevant legislation.

7   Name two different products in your establishment and find out what storage instructions the producers give.

   ....

   ....

8   What policy has your organisation regarding complying with the legal requirements of the storage of goods?

   ....

9   At what temperature should the following equipment be maintained?

   Refrigerator: 5°C   Meat cabinet: ....

   Fish cabinet: ....   Freezer: ....

Stock rotation procedures are fully maintained.

10   Why is this so important with perishable foods?

....

11   Is rotation of tinned stock necessary? If your answer is 'yes', state why.

....

Deterioration and losses of stock in storage are identified and investigated, the appropriate remedial action is taken and/or reported.

12   Name two commodities which deteriorate and explain why deterioration occurs.

....

....

13   Why may stock be 'lost'?

....

14   Explain how deterioration and loss may be prevented.

....

....

15   What action would you take in your establishment to prevent deterioration?

....

....

Security of stock is maintained by appropriate procedures.

16   What procedure is in force to ensure that stock is secure within your organisation?

....

....

17 Name four of the storekeepers roles with regard to security.

   a Accurate record keeping

   b ....

   c ....

   d ....

18 What physical conditions are necessary and what procedures must be complied with to make stores safe and secure?

   ....

   ....

19 What do you understand by spot check and full check?

   ....

   ....

20 Access to stock and the use of space is optimised. Suggest how access to stock is achieved:
   By the design of stores:

   ....

   By the siting of stores:

   ....

   By fittings in stores:

   ....

21 Who is responsible for using storage space advantageously?

   ....

Opportunities to improve the storage system are identified and recommendations made to the appropriate authority.

22 In what ways can the existing storage system in your establishment be improved?

....

....

23 To whom would you make recommendations and how would you present them?

....

....

24 If you thought 'sack the storekeeper', how would you express such an idea?

....

Relevant information is accurately recorded in the appropriate format and made available to the appropriate people.

25 Name seven items of information regarding stock that need to be recorded.

a Amount received   **e** ....

b Amount issued   **f** ....

c ....   **g** ....

d ....

26 What system of records exists in your organisation?

....

....

27 Who in your establishment needs to know the details of stock used, stock in hand and stock required?

....

....

28 Name two computer software packages that are available as a food and beverage stock control system.

....

....

29 The key objective of storage is to ensure that an adequate supply of all purchased items is maintained for immediate use, with the minimum loss arising from wastage, spoilage or p............................

30 In order to ensure the correct storage procedures are followed, it is important that:

a The stores are well designed, to ensure no access to .... personnel.

b Shelves are of the .... specification.

c Each storage area is maintained at the .... temperature.

d Opening times of some storage areas may be r..............................

31 A key point of the storage function is the maintenance of clerical records. These may be in the form of:

a Stock book

b B.......... cards

c Stock cards

The objective is to accurately record all stock movements in and out of the store.

32 A vital part is ensuring the accuracy of the stock records and the physical stock take.

This must be done when ....

and must be independently ....

When the stocktaking process is complete and the appropriate stock levels computed, it is vital to know what the level of stock should be.

33 The optimum stock level should relate directly to the known consumption pattern but should take into account:

a The maximum consumption of a product against the m......................... re-order time.

b the usual length of the re......................... cycle.

c The economic .... to be ordered.

d Delivery ....

e Storage .... available

f The shelf .... of ....

g Purchase terms available at the time of ordering.

h Cash .... constraints

i Price .... and .... demand.

3B2.3 *Control of the issue of stock/goods*

Stock/goods are issued on receipt of the appropriate authorisation and/or documentation.

1 What documents are required in your establishment before goods are issued from stores?

    ....

    ....

2 Who has authority to:
    Issue goods?

    ....

    Request goods?

    ....

3 Are there any restrictions on, for example, specific goods or certain amounts, which may be requisitioned in your organisation?

    ....

    ....

4 What information is needed on a requisition form?

    ....

    ....

5 What do you understand by countersigned?

....

....

Goods issued match specific requirements.

6 Why should goods issued be the same as those requested?

....

....

7 If items cannot be supplied from stores or only partially supplied, what is the procedure in your establishment?

....

....

Goods are issued in accordance with stock rotation procedures and organisational policy.

8 Who issues goods which are requested and in what order are items issued from stock?

....

....

9 What is the organisational procedure with which you or your colleagues comply?

....

....

Records of issues are complete, accurate and made available to the appropriate people.

10 Who may be responsible for keeping records?

....

11 How must records be kept?

....

....

12 Who has access to records?

....

CONTROL OF SUBSTANCES HAZARDOUS TO HEALTH REGULATIONS 1988

The Control of Substances Hazardous to Health Regulations 1988 (COSHH) came into effect on 1 October 1989 and place a duty on all employers to reduce employee exposure to hazardous substances to within, and preferably below, acceptable limits. The emphasis is on personal, as opposed to environmental, exposure and consideration should be given to skin contact, skin absorption, inhalation and ingestion.

All employers have a duty to ensure comprehensive assessments are carried out for every identifiable substance hazardous to health encountered at work.

13 What should the assessment cover?
  a Identification of all substances hazardous to health associated with the work processes.

  b Employees likely to be ....

  c Degree and length of ....

  d Work areas affected.

  e Existing control m............................. and their efficiency.

  f Existing monitoring ....

  g Existing provision for in............................. information and training.

  h Recommendations for any inadequacies.

14 Who should carry out the assessment?

....

3B2.4 *Implement the physical stock-take within the area of responsibility*

When presenting information, having made a physical stock-take it may be essential to clarify certain factors. Examples of this could be explanations of why items have been damaged or deteriorated. All items of stock have value, but if they have not yet been paid for, this information should be made known as would items for which a credit note has been issued. Materials and goods used for display, exhibitions, competitions, etc., would be noted and accounted for. Information about future issues needs to be included so as to complete the picture, and orders may be in but not yet issued.

Should stock be transferred to other departments, branches or stores, this information needs to be recorded and passed to those in the establishment who need to be informed. It is essential that the physical stock-take and the records agree. Any reconciliation should be stated so as to explain the discrepancy between actual goods and the stock-take records.

Stock-taking procedures are effectively communicated to the appropriate staff.

1 Why should those persons responsible for stock know what procedures are required of them for stock-taking?

    ....

    ....

2 In what form can communication be most effective?

    ....

Required documentation is made available to the appropriate staff.

3 State three documents which would be required.

    ....

4 Explain the purpose of these documents.

    ....

    ....

    ....

5 Who may be the appropriate staff requiring the documents?

....

Records of physical stock-take are complete, accurate and up to date.

6 Why should records be accurate, complete and up to date?

....

....

Additional information which will affect stock reconciliation is made available to the appropriate people.

7 Give four examples which may affect stock reconciliation.

....

....

....

....

8 Who may require this information?

....

All relevant information is accurately recorded in a suitable format and made available to the appropriate people.

9 What information is required when stock-taking?

....

Record of Achievement – Completion of Unit 3B2

Candidate's signature   ....

Assessor's signature   ....

Date   ....

Unit 3D1

Monitor and maintain the health, safety and security of workers, customers and other members of the public

Read *Advanced Practical Cookery* pages 12–15.

3D1.1 *Maintain security/safety procedures in own area of responsibility*

1 How would you identify potential security risks in areas for which you are responsible?

....

....

2 What procedure would you follow, having discovered faults in the security system?

....

....

3 Why is it necessary for employees to be security conscious?

....

....

4 In your establishment, how frequently are inspections carried out regarding security of premises?

....

5 List the potential lapses of security which may occur.

....

....

6 Hazard spotting is necessary to prevent accidents. What hazards can you spot in your working environment?

....

....

7 What procedures do you take to prevent there being hazardous situations?

....

....

8 In the event of an accident occurring, to whom should it be reported and where recorded?

....

....

9 What is the policy in your establishment for ensuring accidents and lapses in security are reported and appropriate action taken?

....

....

10 What details are to be recorded following an accident?

....

....

11 Equipment manufacturers produce instructions for use. What other information may they provide?

....

....

12 Why should manufacturers' guidelines be followed?

....

13 What information should be sited by electrical cutting and slicing equipment?

....

....

14 Who should be informed when there is a serious accident?

....

15 Who is responsible for first aid in your workplace?

....

16 Where is your nearest accident and emergency hospital department?

....

3D1.2 *Monitor and maintain the health and safety of workers, customers and other members of the public*

1 List the categories of people entering the premises who could be at risk where you work.

....

....

2 What potential risks could endanger these people?

....

....

3 What routines occur to ensure that premises are free from hazards and have high standards of hygiene?

....

....

4 How frequently should safety and maintenance checks take place?

....

5 Why should details of an accident be recorded and why should it be legible?

....

....

6 Why should equipment instructions be fully complied with?

....

....

7 What health and safety signs may be required and how should they be displayed?

....

....

8 Explain why maintenance checks are necessary. How are faults rectified and by whom?

....

....

....

....

9 Where in your establishment is the first aid box and what are its contents?

....

....

10 Name two organisations who run first aid courses.

....

....

11 Explain the procedure for treating cuts and burns.

....

....

....

12 State the major causes of accidents in kitchens.

....

....

3D1.3 *Maintain a healthy and safe working environment*

1 How do staff in your establishment know the legislation regarding health and safety?

....

2 What methods are employed to ensure compliance with the health and safety legislation?

....

....

3 Explain how hazards can be avoided.

....

....

4 Having obtained a safe and healthy working environment, how can this situation be continued?

....

....

5 Why is training in health and safety essential and what should it include?

....

....

6 Where would you obtain information regarding fire prevention and procedures in the event of a fire?

....

....

7 In the event of a bomb alert, what is your organisation's policy and procedure?

....

....

8 What records regarding health and safety must be kept and what details should they contain?

....

....

....

9 What procedures should occur in the event of:
   a Infestation

....

....

   b Contamination

....

....

10 What happens in your establishment when staff fail to comply with the organisation's standards?

....

....

11   Why is ongoing training regarding health and safety essential?

....

....

12   Explain why all areas accessible to staff and other persons must be safe.

....

....

Record of Achievement – Completion of Unit 3D1

Candidate's signature   ....

Assessor's signature   ....

Date   ....

PATISSERIE AND
CONFECTIONERY

Prepare and cook complex
hot and cold desserts

3NF1.1 *Prepare complex hot desserts*
3NF1.2 *Cook and finish complex hot desserts*

Read *Advanced Practical Cookery* pages 461–70.

Food hygiene is essential when working in the pastry and bakery environment.

1   State six basic principles of food hygiene that you observe when working in this
    department.
    Example   All items are stored correctly in accordance with the required legislation.

    ....

    ....

    ....

    ....

    ....

    ....

2   Employees are also responsible for safety under the Health and Safety Act. Outline
    how you implement the safety policy within the department.

    ....

    ....

3   Name three processes in the pastry kitchen which are most likely to kill food
    poisoning bacteria.

    ....

    ....

    ....

4   A classical apple charlotte is unmoulded and served hot. What precautions have to be taken in order that the product does not collapse on unmoulding?

   ....

   ....

5   Name six hot sweets with which you are familiar.

   ....

   ....

   ....

6   Describe the preparation, cooking and service of two of the above sweets. Sketch the suitable plate service of one of the described sweets.

7   Soufflés, pudding soufflé, soufflé pancakes are all aerated hot sweets. What is meant by aerated?

   ....

8 What is a panada?

....

9 How are the following flavours added to a panada for soufflé?
       Chocolate:

....

       Grand Marnier:

....

       Coffee:

....

10 What is added to egg white in order to strengthen it, e.g. for beating?

....

11 How does a pancake differ from a waffle?

....

12 List six pancake fillings and three waffle fillings.

....

....

....

....

....

13 Maple syrup is often served with waffles, but what is maple syrup?

....

14 At what temperature should a four-portion soufflé be cooked?

....

15 Describe a soufflé of your own choice, one which you have prepared or have seen
       prepared in your establishment, which is not a classical recipe.

....

....

16 Why is strong flour used in the production of apple strudel?

....

17 Name three variations to apple strudel.

....

....

18 Give the recipe based on four to six portions for a classical steamed sponge pudding.

....

....

....

19 Describe four hot sweets using steamed sponge pudding mix for plated service which do not follow classical lines. Illustrate your answer with sketches.

20 Name the various types of rice used for hot sweets.

....

21 How does a French rice pudding differ from a traditional English rice pudding?

....

22 Describe four hot sweets with which you are familiar where the main ingredient is cereal based.

....

....

....

....

23 Suggest a suitable rice-, semolina- or tapioca-based hot sweet which could be suitable for banquet service. How would you serve it for 250 people?

....

....

24 Describe how hot sweets may be modified to take account of healthy eating.

....

....

25 Outline the quality control points essential when writing standardised recipes for hot sweets.

a Purchasing; specification of ingredients correct.

b Preparation procedures; correct storage temperature; handling.

c ....

d ....

e ....

f ....

26 Give examples of hot sweet dishes which use the following preparations.

Preparation	Hot sweet
Creaming	Steamed sponge pudding ....
Use of moulds	Pudding soufflé ....
Folding	Omelette soufflé Jalousie ....
Incorporating fat	Apple turnover ....
Aeration	French rice pudding ....

27 Outline the main contamination threats that are likely when preparing hot sweets.

....

....

....

28 What storage precautions should be taken when preparing uncooked hot sweets?

    a That they are stored at the correct temperature.

    b ....

    c ....

    d ....

29 Name a hot sweet which may be finished by one of the following methods:

Finish	Hot sweet
Grilling	Flan viennoise
Turning out, de-moulding	
Cooling	
Glazing	
Coating	
Filling	Pancakes
Piping	
Dipping	
Sprinkling	
Portioning	Apple strudel

30 State the common faults often to be found in the following sweets:

Hot sweet	Common faults
Soufflé	Oven too cool Insufficient beating of egg whites Overbeating of egg whites ....

Hot sweet	Common faults
Rice pudding	Ingredients weighed incorrectly; too much rice giving a heavy, stodgy texture ....
Sponge puddings	Mixture too wet ....
Choux paste fritters	Deep-frying oil not at correct temperature ....
Apple fritters	Batter runs off; apple ring should have been passed through flour then batter ....

31 Suggest a different hot sweet which may be produced from the following fruits:

Fruit	Hot sweet
Fresh strawberries	
Fresh rhubarb	
Fresh blackcurrants	
Fresh gooseberries	
Fresh peaches	
Dried apricots	
Fresh mangoes	

32 With two of the fresh fruits and the hot sweets you have listed in question 31, describe their preparation, cooking, finish and service.

....

....

....

....

33 Classic 'charlotte portugaise' is served warm/hot.
a What type of flavour would you add to the sponge mix?

....

b State the recommended filling and briefly describe the method of production.

....

....

c Present a product sketch for a one or four portion charlotte portugaise, indicating clearly the composition.

34 If only fresh egg white was available, describe a suitable method to produce the meringue and finishing the charlotte portugaise, conforming to the new regulations.

....

....

....

....

....

....

35 When using couverture chocolate for a soufflé, the chocolate should NOT be boiled up with the milk. Briefly explain why!

....

....

....

36 Describe the method of production, baking and serving of a fruit purée based soufflé.

....

....

....

....

....

....

....

....

....

....

37 What is the most suitable type of 'sponge product' to be cut into cubes and soaked with liqueur and then added to soufflé mixes? State a reason why.

....

....

....

....

38 Describe the method of production and service for an 'omelette soufflé'.

....

....

....

....

....

....

39 Explain how you would fill the dishes when making 'soufflé arlequin', stating the main effect required when presenting the baked soufflé.

....

....

....

40 **a** What does the term 'mousseux' denote when examining the texture of a cooked soufflé?

....

b What °C should the core temperature be to conform with today's regulations?

....

41 Briefly explain the composition and method of making, baking and serving of crêpe soufflés.

....

....

....

....

....

....

42 a Describe one method by which you could keep cooked pudding soufflés in serving condition during the service period.

....

....

b What are the general reasons given for:

serving pudding soufflé at lunch?

....

....

serving soufflés at dinner?

....

....

43 There are a number of different products on the market under the heading 'strudel', but not made with the conventional strudel paste. Describe one such 'imitation strudel', stating the ingredients and method of production, baking and serving.

....

....

....

....

44 Is 'pear flan bourdalou' normally served warm or hot?

....

a Describe the basic composition of the flan.

....

....

....

....

b List two other flans/tarts which are normally served warm or hot. Explain the composition for one of the chosen flans.

....

....

....

....

....

....

45 Explain what a 'beignet soufflé surprise' is and suggest a suitable sauce to be served with it.

....

....

....

46 Describe two desserts made using suet paste as the main ingredient and explain how you would serve them plated and with a sauce.

....

....

....

....

....

....

....

....

....

....

....

....

....

....

....

....

3NF1.3 *Prepare complex cold desserts*
3NF1.4 *Process and cook complex cold desserts*

Read *Advanced Practical Cookery* pages 470–92.

1   Outline four main hygiene procedures which have to be followed when preparing
    cold sweets relevant to current legislation.
    Example   Due care is taken to make sure that all risk of contamination is minimised
    through careful handling, preparation and storage of raw materials.

....

....

....

....

....

2   How should cold sweets which contain large amounts of fresh cream be stored?

....

....

....

3 Name a cold sweet using each of the following preparation methods.

Preparation method	Cold sweet
Creaming	
Folding	
Aeration	Cold lemon soufflé
Using the addition of flavours and colours	
Combining	

4 Describe the method of preparation and service of two of the sweets and give the amounts for 20 covers.

....

....

....

....

....

....

....

5 Gelatine is a natural setting agent produced from collagen. Give a vegetarian alternative.

....

6 Fonds are commercial mousse preparations which are ideally suited to bulk production. These fonds often use a mixture of setting agents to give a smooth high-quality mouth feel gel. Name four different setting agents used in fonds.

....

....

7   Describe the use of jaconde mixture in the production of cold sweets.

....

....

8   Either draw the presentation of one sweet you have produced recently from a jaconde mixture, or using your creativity and imagination create a sweet using the mixture.

9   State the reasons for using silpat mats in preference to silicone paper when making two-coloured jaconde biscuits.

....

....

10   Why is it necessary to adjust the recipe for a chocolate bavarois if using a 70–72 per cent cocoa solids couverture in place of cooking chocolate?

....

....

11 When making a classic chocolate mousse with a pastry cream base and high in chocolate content, what adjustments would you make to ensure a soft and light texture?

....

....

12 Create two cold sweets suitable for banquet service from the following list only: flour, butter, eggs, sugar, milk, honey, yoghurt, cream cheese, gelatine, flaked almonds, liqueur, fresh pears, apples, mangoes, fresh coconut. Draw the presentation and list the ingredients and method for four portions.

13 Give a costing for one of the sweets.

Name of dish:			Four portions	
Ingredients	Amount	Cost per unit	Cost	
			£	p
		Total cost		
		Cost of one portion		

14 Name six items made in the pastry kitchen using rice grains.
Example   Imperial rice (*Riz à l'impératrice*)

a ....   **d** ....

b ....   **e** ....

c ....   **f** ....

15 List the ingredients of two of the dishes you have mentioned in question 14 and describe the method of production.

....

....

....

....

....

....

....

....

16 State the name of the enzyme in pineapple which reacts with gelatine, making the production of mousse using fresh pineapple and gelatine impossible.

....

17 Describe the action of this protolytic enzyme and gelatine.

....

....

18 Name four cold sweets using meringue.
Example Vacherin aux fruits

a .... **c** ....

b .... **d** ....

19 State the hygiene principles which must be observed when producing meringue.

....

....

20 Why is lemon juice, tartaric acid or acetic acid sometimes added to egg white for the production of meringues?

....

21 How are meringue nests prepared and cooked?

....

....

22 Why may egg white powder be added to egg white for the production of meringue?

....

23 State the hygiene and safety principles that must be observed when using eggs for cold sweets.

....

....

24 If you were inducting an apprentice in the pastry department, outline the safety procedures you would expect him/her to observe; in particular, explain the food safety procedures relating to fresh cream and the finishing of cold sweets.

....

....

....

....

....

....

....

....

....

....

....

....

....

....

25 Describe the process required in the production of:
   Cream-based ice-cream:

   ....

   ....

   A fruit-based water ice:

   ....

   ....

26 List all the ingredients required and describe the making and serving of a red wine sorbet and a red wine granité. Describe the difference between a sorbet and a granité.

   ....

   ....

   ....

   ....

   ....

   ....

27 Draw and label a two-flavoured ice-cream bombe.

28 List the ingredients for a pâte à bombe.

....

....

....

....

29 Show how a pâte à bombe can be used in the making of either a biscuit glacé or soufflé glacé.

....

....

30 Using your creativity, describe by use of a diagram how you would present a biscuit glacé or a soufflé glacé to ensure ease of service and efficient cost/portion control.

31 Ice-cream is a complex emulsion. What is meant by the term emulsion?

....

32 Why is glycerol monostearate added to commercial ice-cream and which substance is used for the same purpose if ice-cream is produced in the pastry department?

....

....

33 Outline the food safety requirements which must be applied to the preparation, production and service of ice-cream goods.

....

....

34 State why fruit/water ice does not freeze to a firm state.

....

35 Explain what causes the granular texture of ice-cream.

....

36 Give a recipe for a cold cheesecake and list six different types of toppings which you are familiar with.

....

....

....

....

....

....

....

37 State the difference between a Chartreuse and a Charlotte.

....

....

38 Name three Chartreuses and three Charlottes with which you are familiar; briefly describe each.

Chartreuse	Description	Charlotte	Description
Banana	Mould lined with lemon jelly, topped with sliced banana, filled with vanilla bavarois	Russe	Mould lined with biscuit à la cuillère, filled with vanilla bavarois

39 Name two cold sweets that use the following basic pastes, giving a brief description. One example for each is given.

Paste	Sweet	Description
Choux paste	Salambos	Large bun filled with rum pastry cream topped with caramel
Puff pastry	Millefeuille	Layers of puff paste filled with cream and fruit
Sweet paste	Pear flan	Sweet paste flan cooked blind, filled with pastry cream and pears glazed with suitable flan jelly

Paste	Sweet	Description
Sablé paste	Raspberry sablé	Rounds of sablé paste filled with raspberries and cream

40 From the following lists, either name or create cold sweets using fresh fruit and pastry.

Fruit	**Pastes**
Apples	Short ....
Blackcurrants	Sweet .... `
Kiwi	Choux ....
Pineapple	Puff ....
Raspberries	Sablé ....

41 Describe two sweets from your answer in question 40, the method of preparation, cooking and serving. Suggest if the sweets mentioned are suitable for banquet service.

....

....

....

....

....

....

....

....

42 Name a cold sweet which may be produced from the following process methods.

Process method	Sweet
Freezing	Biscuit glacé
Boiling	
Baking	
De-moulding	
Refrigeration	

43 Name a cold sweet that may be finished by the following methods:

Finishing method	Cold sweet
Cooling	
Stacking	
Glazing	Crème brulée
Cutting	
Filling	Profiteroles
Piping	Bavarois
Portioning	

44 Name four sweets which can be produced from eggs, milk, cream and sugar using the process poaching *au bain marie*.

....

....

45 Poaching *au bain marie* using the ingredients in question 44 requires special attention during the cooking process. Why?

....

....

46 What is meant by syneresis?

....

47 State how the ingredients for cold sweets can be adjusted to comply with healthy eating guidelines.

....

....

48 Create or modify two existing cold sweet dishes to make them more attractive to the health conscious customer.

....

....

....

....

49 Today's pâtissiers use chocolate meringue bases for a selection of cold sweets.
a List the required ingredients and outline a suitable method of production, including baking temperature and time, and the correct storage procedure for chocolate meringue bases.

....

....

....

b Briefly explain the composition and presentation for one of your chocolate meringue based desserts, using a product sketch to illustrate your answer.

50 Based on classical references, explain
  a the composition of a fruit purée based water ice

  ....

  ....

  b a white wine sorbet

  ....

  ....

51 Briefly explain the composition and two different methods in making a 'pâte à bombe'.

  ....

  ....

  ....

  ....

  ....

  ....

  ....

  ....

  ....

  ....

52 Utilising 'pâte à bombe' in a mousse mixture,
  a list the remaining ingredients required;

  ....

  ....

  ....

  ....

b explain the method of preparation for such a mousse.

....

....

....

....

53 Describe a type of mousse you could make without the use of gelatine. State any change of ingredients and/or method of preparation required for the suggested product.

....

....

....

....

54 Your head chef asks you to suggest a quality cold sweet for a special party, and requires the following information from you:
  a A list of all ingredients needed and an approximate food cost.

....

....

....

....

....

....

....

....

....

....

....

....

....

b The method of preparation and presentation of the sweet, written out in easy to follow stages, illustrated with a product sketch and/or a photograph.

3NF1.5 *Produce sauces, fillings and coatings*

1   Describe the method of making sauce anglaise and state to what degree it must be heated to conform to the current legislation.

....

....

....

....

2   Pastry cream is also sometimes known as confectioners custard. This filling is used for several sweets, it is often flavoured with liqueurs. Name four cold sweets which use pastry cream as a filling, stating if any additional flavours or liqueurs are added to the cream.

Sweet	Pastry cream flavour
Banana flan	Rum pastry cream

3   The filling for a classical gâteau St Honoré is known as a crème chibouste. Describe a crème chibouste and state the required process for the inclusion of egg white.

....

....

....

....

4   Name four items which can be added to fresh cream before sale to the public in accordance with the Cream Regulations 1970.

....

....

5 Describe how starch forms a gel. Name the best starch for use in a jam sauce and give reasons for this.

....

....

6 What are pectins?

....

....

7 What are alginates?

....

....

8 Give an example of the use of alginates in pastry. Relate your answer to a filling, sauce or coating.

....

....

9 Give an example of using a sabayon in hot or cold sweets.

....

10 State the hygiene precautions and procedures which have to be considered when preparing a sabayon. Mention in your answer temperature control and storage.

....

....

....

11 Describe the production of fruit coulis, and outline the different preparation from producing a coulis from hard and soft fruit.

....

....

....

....

12   Suggest a suitable fruit coulis to serve with the following sweets.

Sweet	Coulis
Millefeuille filled with fresh raspberries	
Mango and coconut mousse	
Vacherin filled with marron glacé	
Sablé biscuit filled with kiwi and orange segments, topped with crisp caramel	
Hot vanilla and almond soufflé	
Steamed orange sponge pudding	
Hot glazed peaches wrapped in filo pastry	
Apple and cherry strudel	

13   Complete the recipe for boiled butter cream.

   2 eggs
   50 g (2 oz) icing sugar
   300 g (12 oz) granulated sugar
   100 g (4 oz)
   50 g (2 oz)
   400 g (1 lb)

14   To what temperature should the sugar be boiled for boiled butter cream?

   ....

15   Give three uses of boiled butter cream.

   ....

   ....

16   Describe the use of ganache as a filling and as a coating.

   ....

   ....

17   By the use of a sketch, suggest a combination of fillings in a sweet/dessert that you are familiar with.

18   Describe how to stabilise and store crème chantilly.

   ....

   ....

   ....

19   Outline the basic principle of jam as a preserve.

   ....

   ....

   ....

20 Give four uses of jam as a filling or topping to hot or cold sweets of your choice.

....

....

....

....

21 What chemical preservative is added to commercial jams.

....

22 List any commercially manufactured fillings that you are aware of.

....

....

....

23 What are the advantages of using a high methoxyl pectin glaze?

....

....

24 Compare a fresh-fruit glaze and a pectin glaze.

....

....

25 Identify the glazes or finishes to the following sweets.

Sweet	Finish
Flan Viennoise	
Apple flan	
Strawberry torte	
Tranche Parisienne	
Dartois aux amandes	
Gâteau Japonaise	

26 Now list six sweets of your own choice. Describe the presentation, filling and finish of each.

Sweet	Presentation	Filling	Finish

27 Coulis are often produced from a process of liquidising and blending. Name a sauce, a filling or coating produced from the following processes.

Reducing: ....

Emulsifying: ....

28 Consider how alternative ingredients may be used to introduce a more healthy eating diet for those who require it. How can the fat content of a filling be reduced?

....

....

....

....

29 Using your creativity and imagination, suggest some suitable sauces from the following ingredients suitable to serve with a range of hot or cold sweets.

Orange juice   Coconut
Earl Grey Tea   Sugar
Whisky   Milk
Eggs   Cream
Honey   Fresh limes
Golden syrup   Passion fruit
Cinnamon   Lychees

....

....

....

....

....

....

30 Describe the coating consistency of:
Ganache:

....

Butter cream:

....

Royal icing:

....

31 Why is consistency an important factor in sauce production?

....

....

32 How can each of these be rectified if their consistency is too thin or too thick?

....

....

....

33 When producing coating and fillings, why should the pastry cook be concerned about humidity and temperature?

....

....

34 What are the contamination threats in relation to the making of sauces, filling and coating?
  a Insufficient temperatures reached to destroy bacteria.

  b Pastry cooks contaminating products by poor hygiene techniques.

  c ....

  d ....

  e ....

  f ....

35 Describe, in easy to follow stages, the composition and production method for a 'crème mousseline'. Name two products/dishes using 'crème mousseline'.

....

....

....

....

....

....

....

....

....

....

....

....

....

....

....

....

....

....

....

36 Piping ganache for fine decorative piping can be made from a selection of raw materials. List the required ingredients and the methods for making two such piping ganaches.

....

....

....

....

....

....

....

....

....

....

....

....

....

....

....

....

....

....

37 Dry 'fond' mixes are a combination of different ingredients. Depending on the product brand, all are used to make cold set mousse type fillings.

Name three of the components (raw materials) included in the 'fond' powder with which you are familiar.

....

....

....

....

....

....

Describe the method used to make a mousse type filling with your brand of 'fond', including temperatures of ingredients and mixing times.

....

....

....

....

....

....

Record of Achievement – Completion of Unit 3NFI

Candidate's signature ....

Assessor's signature ....

Date ....

Prepare, cook and finish complex pastry products

3NF2.1 *Prepare and process fresh pastry*
3NF2.2 *Cook and finish complex pastry products*

Read *Advanced Practical Cookery* pages 457–60.

The method in which fat is added to flour in the production of fresh paste affects the overall finished product.

1   Give an example of a paste which may be produced from each of the following:

   Boiling: ....

   Rubbing in: ....

   Creaming: ....

   Lamination: ....

2   Acid is added in the production of puff pastry. The acid acts, upon the gluten, making it more pliable, more extensive, and improving its ability to retain s............................. generated in the baking process; hence pastry is lighter and greater in ....

3   Name the acids which may be added to puff pastry.

   ....

   ....

4   In commercial puff pastry, an enzyme is often added in place of an acid to ensure maximum extensibility of the gluten. Name this enzyme.

   ....

5   Briefly describe how puff pastry rises in the oven.

   ....

   ....

6 What is the relationship between the elasticity of the gluten and the resting time?

....

....

7 What do you understand by the term 'hydrogenated fat'?

....

8 Why does puff pastry made with all pastry margarine look white and stale in a much shorter time than paste containing a good percentage of butter?

....

....

9 Describe the different ways of incorporating fat for the production of puff pastry. It is advisable to show this in diagrammatic form.

10 List two effects on the finished product if:
Puff paste is rolled out in too much flour:

....

Finished puff paste is stored in a warm kitchen:

....

....

Dough is firmer than the butter when folding in the butter.

....

....

11 Name six products which may be produced from short pastry.

....

....

....

12 When making hot water paste, how is the fat incorporated into the flour?

....

....

13 How does hot water paste differ from raised pie paste in its method of production?

....

....

14 Why is hot water paste or raised pie paste best for pork and veal fillings?

....

....

15 Why do pork pies, jellied with agar agar, go off less quickly than those jellied with gelatine or with meat stock?

....

....

16 Give a recipe for a wholemeal short pastry.

....

....

....

....

....

....

....

....

17 List four products where shortening can replace other fats or oils.

....

....

18 Give the factors which control the volume of choux pastry.

a When choux paste is being baked, any air that has been beaten into it will expand and the water in the paste will be converted into steam.

b The expanded air as well as the steam tries to escape from the paste but is mostly prevented from doing so because both are trapped and retained within the paste by films of c............................ gluten and unc............................ films of egg ....

c Egg albumen is extensible and will be in............................ and distended by the internal .... of the gases .... and .... thus the pastries increase a v............................ and expansion only ceases when the egg albumen films use their extensibility and .... powers. However, the moisture which is near to the surface of the paste is driven off fairly quickly, after which the temperature of this water layer of paste, can rise well above the temperature of boiling water.

d During the latter part of this period, and as the paste has already reached very considerable volume, the egg proteins are c............................. and set.

e The volume of the choux pastry goods will depend only slightly upon the strength and extensibility of the gluten of the flour, but very largely upon the gas-holding power of the egg proteins.

19 It is essential to create steam within the paste, under sufficient pressure to aerate as much as possible before coagulation of proteins and surface drying or crust-formation occur. This, however, can only be achieved in what temperature oven?

....

20 Egg albumen is mainly responsible for the ultimate volume of choux paste. Is the strength of the flour of equal importance?

....

21 When making choux paste, why should the eggs never be beaten into the panada until it has been partially or completely cooled?

....

....

22 Why is vol (ammonium carbonate) sometimes added to commercially produced choux paste?

....

....

23 Name four afternoon tea pastries produced from choux pastry.

....

....

24 What is meant by 'fraiser' the paste? What is its purpose?

....

....

25 Give a recipe for sweet pastry using the four ratio numbers which correspond to quantities of ingredients – 8:4:2:1.

....

....

....

....

26 Create a product of your own choice suitable as an afternoon pastry or as a sweet using either puff paste, short paste or sweet paste or a combination of these. Illustrate your answer by use of diagrams.

27 Give the possible reasons for faults which may occur to short pastry.
Hard:

....

....

Soft-crumbly:

....

....

Blistered:

....

....

Soggy:

....

....

Shrunken:

....

....

28 Give the possible reason for faults in puff pastry.
Not flaky:

....

....

Fat oozes out:

....

Hard:

....

....

Shrunken:

....

....

Soggy:

....

....

Uneven rise:

....

....

29 Name three uses of sweet paste.

....

....

30 Give the possible reasons for faults in sweet paste.
Heavy and soggy:

....

Tough:

....

31 How should strudel paste be stretched?

....

....

32   Give four uses for sablé paste.

....

....

33   How does noodle paste differ from ravioli paste?

....

....

34   What relationship does strudel paste have with filo paste?

....

....

35   Give four uses for filo paste.

....

....

36   Create a recipe of your own choice using filo paste. The recipe should be suitable for banquet service. Give an outline costing for 10 covers.

....

....

....

....

....

....

....

....

37 Name two types of oven suitable for efficient baking of all pastry and most basic baking products.

....

38 Outline the basic hygiene principles that have to be observed when making fresh pastes.

....

....

....

....

39 Name a paste or product which may be produced using the following preparation methods.

Preparation method	Paste
Mixing	
Folding	Puff pastry Rough puff pastry
Cutting	
Relaxing	All basic pastes
Kneading	
Incorporating fat	All basic pastes
Conducting/chilling	
Scraping down	Sablé paste

40 Using a diagram, show the difference between notching and crimping.

41 From the diagram below, explain what has happened during the baking of the flan case.

....

....

....

....

42   From the following cooking methods, suggest a product that may be produced using fresh paste.

Cooking methods	Product
Baking with filling	Dartois from puff pastry
Steaming	
Boiling/poaching	Gnocchi from choux pastry
Baking blind	
Deep frying	

43   There are many different ways of finishing goods produced from fresh pastry. Name two products which use the following techniques.

Finish	Product
Glazing	....
Piping	....
Dusting	Apple strudel ....
Filling	Profiteroles (choux pastry) ....
Dripping	....
Enrobing	....
Portioning	Millefeuille (puff pastry) ....
Use of heat gun	Caramelising Flan viennoise – short pastry

44 Name any other finishing method which you have used which is not listed in question 43.

....

45 What is high ratio fat?

....

46 How does hydrogenated fat differ from high ratio fat?

....

....

47 List the advantages and disadvantages which have to be considered when you purchase commercial paste, such as frozen puff paste.

....

....

....

....

....

....

48 List any commercial paste/products used by your establishment and assess their quality and performance.

....

....

....

....

....

....

49 Explain how recipes for fresh paste may be adapted to make them more 'healthy'.

....

....

50 Suggest ways in which trimmings can be minimised when preparing and using fresh paste.

....

....

51 List any bad practices you have observed in the storage of paste and also in dealing with trimmings.

....

....

....

....

52 Outline the relevant health and safety and food hygiene legislation relating to the production of fresh paste.

....

....

....

....

53 When lining flans with puff paste for sweet or savoury products, explain the three main points to be observed to obtain finished products of consistently good standard.

....

....

....

54 Describe briefly the function of a 'tartelette' machine.

....

Outline the three points which need to be checked before using the tartelette machine.

....

....

....

55 State the percentage of fat in

a dairy butter..

b puff pastry margarine ....

How much pastry margarine would you recommend to use for 1 kg flour mix when making a 'full puff paste'?

....

56 Describe the mouth feel after tasting puff paste made with a pastry margarine where the melting point was 32–34°C.

....

State the melting points in °C for butter and good quality puff pastry margarine.

....

57 Describe the differences between the following types of 'flours':

a flour made from summer wheat – flour made from winter wheat

....

b White strong/bread flour – standard cake flour

....

c Wholewheat flour – white strong flour

....

d Cornflour – plain cake flour

....

58 State the possible alterations needed to change a basic 'vanilla sablé paste' recipe to a chocolate sablé paste.

....

....

59 When making an 'almond sablé paste' with 25% of the flour weight in ground almonds, state which ingredients you would adjust, and how to maintain the texture of the basic sablé paste.

....

....

Record of Achievement – Completion of Unit 3NF2

Candidate's signature ....

Assessor's signature ....

Date ....

Unit 3NF3

Prepare, process and finish complex fermented dough products

Read *Advanced Practical Cookery* pages 504–12.

3NF3.1 *Prepare complex fermented dough products*

3NF3.2 *Process and finish complex fermented dough products*

Yeast goods make use of baker's yeast. Fermentation will only take place with sugar. The flour starch is converted to maltose by flour enzymes which are activated in the presence of water. The maltose is then converted to glucose by maltase which is secreted by the yeast cells. Then other yeast cells convert glucose to carbon dioxide and alcohol. The flour protein undergoes alteration so that the flour will retain the carbon dioxide.

1 Does the size of the starch cells present in flour make any difference to the working of such flour in a dough? Explain fully.

....

....

....

....

Viewed through a microscope, a grain of starch will be found to have a very definite shape, but grains from the same source do look similar. For example, a starch cell of wheat is round or slightly oval in shape, and is larger than some of the other kinds of starch, such as rice.

2 What happens to these starch cells when they become moistened and heated?

....

....

Starches and sugars are carbohydrates which means that they are comprised of three elements, carbon, hydrogen and oxygen, with the latter two elements in proportions necessary to form water. This means that for every atom of oxygen present there will be two atoms of hydrogen. The only difference in the formula for starch and sugar is that the starch contains less water than the sugar, but it is possible to change the former into the latter if it can be induced to take up the extra portion of water.

3 This action is called the hy............................. or sacc............................. of starch.

Dilute acids and some enzymes have the ability to change starch to sugar, and will cause gelatinised starch to combine chemically with extra water so that the starch becomes hydrolysed to sugar.

4 Syneresis is the name given to a particular physical or colloidal change that takes place in starch gels as they age. Give an example of syneresis in relation to flour, yeast and fermentation.

....

....

5 Both yeast and baking powder produce carbon dioxide gas to aerate the materials with which they are mixed, but why is yeast often used in preference to baking powder?

....

....

6 Why is salt used in breadmaking?

....

7 Yeast is a living organism. By what other name is baker's yeast also known?

....

8 Yeast like all other living things must receive sufficient food to enable healthy growth and reproduction to continue. Flour itself normally contains all the foods that are required by yeast for its life and growth. List the conditions required for the yeast to grow and reproduce.

....

....

In a ferment, the yeast acting upon the sugars produces carbon dioxide which first dissolves in the water to produce carbonic acid. When the water is saturated with the gas, further supplies of the gas become enmeshed by the strands of gluten contained in the ferment, blowing them up into tiny balloons. The continued increase in the quantity of gas aerates the whole of the ferment and slowly inflates it. The increasing of the bulk will continue until, in the case of the ferment, the expansion of the gluten becomes so great that it cannot stretch any further. As the supply of gas is still continuing, the tiny balloons burst.

9 What happens to the ferment?

....

....

10 Why is dough kept covered with a cloth or, preferably, polythene?

....

....

11 Why should you use rice dust instead of flour when moulding dough?

....

....

12 Why is it that bun doughs which contain excessive fat and sugar do not produce satisfactory results?

....

....

13 Why do bun products sometimes acquire a wrinkled surface skin after baking?

....

....

14 Explain why bun goods masked with sugar syrup direct from the oven do not become soaked but acquire a shiny, slightly sticky surface.

....

....

15 Why are fat, sugar and fruit not worked into the dough which is required for dough products until the dough has reached its full state of ripeness?

....

....

16 List the main stages of manufacture for the following doughs:
  Bun dough by direct method:

....

....

....

  Bread roll dough by ferment and dough:

....

....

....

17 Describe the texture and general appearance of bread rolls if:
  Made with soft cake flour:

....

....

  The dough is processed green:

....

....

18 With regard to yeast doughs, briefly describe the following terms:
  BFT and ADD:

....

....

  Ripeness:

....

....

Optimum dough temperature:

....

....

19 Give two examples of laminated yeast doughs.

....

20 Describe the difference in strong flour, wholemeal and soft flour.

....

....

21 Describe the following processing techniques:
    Developing the dough:

....

....

Proving the dough:

....

....

Knocking back the dough:

....

....

Dividing the dough:

....

....

Extracting the dough:

....

....

Sheeting and cutting the dough:

....

....

Retarding the dough:

....

....

22   Draw the piece of equipment known as a 'retarder'.

23 Give the method for brioche.

125 ml (¼ pt) milk
25 g (1 oz) yeast
450 g (1 lb 2 oz) strong flour
25 g (1 oz) castor sugar
pinch of salt
50 g (2 oz) butter or margarine
4 eggs
2 g malt extract
zest of 1 lemon
150 g (6 oz) butter or margarine

....

....

....

....

....

....

24 Give three uses of brioche paste.

....

....

25 Using 600 g (1 lb 8 oz) bread flour, give the remainder of the ingredients for croissant.

....

....

....

....

....

....

26 With the use of diagrams, describe the technique of producing the croissant shape.

27 Give a basic recipe for Danish pastry dough.

....

....

....

28 List six types of Danish pastries.

....

....

29 Describe the production of three of the Danish pastries you have named.

....

....

....

....

....

....

30 List the major common faults associated with the production of yeast doughs.

a Insufficient yeast development.

b Under proving.

c ....

d ....

e ....

f ....

g ....

h ....

31 Chollo bread is a traditional Jewish bread. It takes the form of a plait. Listed below is the technique for a four-strand plait. Give the order of sequence for a five-strand plait.

4 strand plait	5 strand plait
2 over 3	....
4 over 2	....
1 over 3	....

32 Give a recipe for a fermented batter.

....

....

....

33 Suggest four uses of a yeast batter.

....

....

34 List the main contamination threats likely to occur when preparing and storing fermented dough products. Suggest how to minimise these risks.

Main Contamination Threats	How to Minimise Risks
Stored in the wrong refrigerator with high odour products that are likely to taint dough.	Store in correct refrigerator away from foods which are likely to taint.

35 Name a yeast product which uses the following finishing methods.

Finishing method	Fermented product
Moulding	
Cutting	
Dusting	Cream buns
Addition of seeds	Bread rolls
Shaping	
Plaiting	Chollo bread
Piping	
Glazing	

36 Discuss ways in which wastage can be minimised during the production of fermented products.

....

....

....

37 State how equipment, small equipment and preparation surfaces should be dealt with when handling fermented goods in line with current legislation.

....

....

....

....

....

....

38 Describe the main quality or property of flour when it

    a   is milled from English wheat.

....

    b   is milled from Canadian spring wheat.

....

    c   is a top patent flour.

....

    d   has a high extraction rate.

....

    e   is best suited to bread, general yeast doughs and puff paste.

....

39 Explain the main differences in composition between a 'brioche dough' and a 'plain bun dough'.

....

40 **a** Name four items which can be made from a 'pâte a baba' (savarin dough)

....

....

b Describe a practical method for making a savarin dough and using it to make up babas and pomponettes.

....

....

c Explain how the texture of a savarin dough differs from that of a bread dough.

....

41 Explain briefly what changes you would have to make to a basic bread roll dough if a bread improver was used.

....

42 With regard to basic yeast dough, state:

a the effect that reducing the yeast in a recipe will have on the process.

....

b the two main purposes of fermentation.

....

c the two conditions necessary in a proving cabinet.

....

43 Describe briefly

a the four factors that may slow fermentation.

....

....

....

....

b two reasons that explain the purpose of 'knocking back' yeast doughs.

....

....

c the main advantage of using ADD (activated dough development)

....

44 Explain the function of two pieces of equipment (not ovens or basic mixer) specially used in the bakery section to process fermented dough products.

....

....

....

Record of Achievement – Completion of Unit 3NF3

Candidate's signature ....

Assessor's signature ....

Date ....

Unit 3NF4

Prepare, process and finish complex cake and sponge products

Read *Advanced Practical Cookery* pages 492–504.

3NF4.1 *Prepare complex cake and sponge products*
3NF4.2 *Process and finish complex cake and sponge products*

1 Why is it essential to use good-quality, medium soft flour in the making of slab cakes by the flour or sugar batter methods?

   a This type of flour has the requisite quality and quantity of gluten.

   b ....

2 A flour having too high a percentage of gluten in its composition will cause unsightly cracks to appear across the tops of baked slab cakes and will make them tough. What type of texture will they have?

....

3 What effect would too low a percentage of gluten have on the slab cakes?

....

4 Why is a cake made with all butter not as good as a cake made with part butter and part 100 per cent fat?

....

....

5 Cake batters sometimes curdle. Why is this?

....

....

6 Why is greaseproof paper treated with a solution of silicone resins now used extensively in baking?

....

....

7 Why must the ingredients contained in a cake mixing be balanced?

....

....

8 What are the effects of the following on a cake mixing?
Too much baking powder:

....

....

Too much sugar:

....

....

Too much liquid:

....

....

9 What three effects does sugar have on a cake apart from as a sweetener?
a Moistening agent.

b ....

c ....

10 When baking cakes, what happens if they are moved or knocked while in the oven?

....

....

11 Give three reasons why cakes sometimes sink in the middle.
    Example   Cake removed from oven before thoroughly cooked.

    ....

    ....

    ....

12 What makes high ratio cake flour different from ordinary flour?

    ....

    ....

13 One of the commonest faults with cherry and fruit cakes is that the fruit sinks to the
    bottom. Give reasons for this.

    ....

    ....

    ....

    ....

14 What effect do ground almonds have on the prevention of fruit sinking when cake
    mixing?

    ....

    ....

15 What else can be added to the cake mixing to prevent fruit from sinking?

    ....

16 As soon as cakes are placed in a hot oven, the heat melts the fats – first on the
    outside, then in the middle. At the same time the air cells begin to expand and if
    baking powders are present carbon dioxide is released, slowly at first, from the
    outside to the inside. What happens to the starch cells as the temperature rises?

    ....

17 List advantages of having the oven filled when baking cakes.
    a If the oven is filled with cakes, the volume of steam given off will be fairly large and will act upon the surfaces of the cakes, keeping them moist.

    b ....

       ....

18 If cakes are placed in a cool oven, aeration proceeds at a good rate, but what effect does this have on the cake?

    ....

    ....

19 When lemon juice is to be added to a cake batter, why is it best to add it after the eggs have been thoroughly mixed in?

    ....

    ....

20 Glycerine is an ingredient which is used in cake mixing; it is known to be hygroscopic. Why use glycerine? What is meant by hygroscopic?

    ....

    ....

    ....

21 Why should rich fruit cakes be stored before being decorated? For how long and in what kind of storage?

    ....

    ....

22 What contamination threats does one have to be aware of when referring to cakes, and how can these threats be minimised?

....

....

....

....

23 Why does the presence of grease destroy the aeration of sponge?

....

....

24 If grease destroys the aeration of sponge batters, an extra light cake can be produced by the addition of melted butter at the time of adding the flour. Why is this?

....

....

25 Why do Swiss rolls sometimes crack when being rolled? Why do chocolate Swiss rolls have a greater tendency to crack?

....

....

26 Why are GMS and other emulsifiers added to commercial Swiss rolls?

....

....

27 A sponge batter containing sugar and 100 per cent fat will take more egg than one which contains sugar and butter or margarine. Explain the effect of water on this.

....

....

28 State the method of producing a sponge using:
The traditional sponge method:

....

....

....

....

An emulsifier:

....

....

....

....

29 State the changes required for correct recipe balance if ground almonds are added to a Swiss roll sheet.

....

....

30 State the approximate percentage by which cornflour can replace flour in a sponge mix. What effect does cornflour have on the mix?

....

....

31 List the types of ingredients which are essential to the success of a high ratio cake mix. How do these ingredients differ from normal types suitable for use in conventional cake mixing?

....

....

....

....

32 Eggs, yeast and chemical raising agents are all used to achieve aeration in baked goods. Explain how the aeration occurs for each and give the conditions necessary for a successful product.

Eggs:

....

....

....

Yeast:

....

....

....

Chemicals:

....

....

....

33 If you are required to use a chocolate sponge pre-mix, how does the production method differ from making a conventional genoise?

....

....

34 Referring to the sponge pre-mix, state the relevance of:

Scaling:

....

....

Baking times:

....

....

Temperatures:

....

....

35 How should the following be stored?
Baking powder:

....

Sheets of baked sponge:

....

36 State the storage problems related to baked goods and general mise-en-place in any establishment or training institution in which you have worked.

....

....

37 How do you think general storage could be improved in relation to any pastry department?

....

....

38 Lucerne fruit and pastry cream roulade is produced from sheets of Swiss roll. Suggest four variations to this recipe and state why this product is suitable for banquets. How should it be stored?

....

....

....

....

....

....

....

....

....

....

39 Give an example of a torten. Using your creativity and imagination, design a torten product. List all the ingredients and describe your produce using a diagram.

40 Give an example of teabread. Suggest a suitable recipe.

....

....

....

....

....

....

....

....

....

41 Name a classic gâteau which may be produced from the ingredients below. Itemise the method of production.

10 whites of egg
200 g (8 oz) ground almonds
25 g (1 oz) cornflour
200 g (8 oz) praline buttercream
50 g (2 oz) chocolate fondant

....

....

....

....

....

....

42 Name three types of sponge or cake product which may be produced from the following methods.

Preparation method	Product
Creaming	Madeira cake ....
Folding	Gâteau Japonaise ....
Rubbing In	Coconut cake ....
Aeration	Genoise ....
Chemical raising agent	Scones ....

43 Give an example when steam is introduced into the baking process and state its purpose.

....

....

....

....

....

44 Name products which are finished using the following methods.

Finishing methods	Product
Glazing	Fruit meringue torte ....
Piping	Gâteau mocha ....
Dusting	Baked cheese cake ....
Portioning	Apple and raisin roulade ....

45 What effect does the following have in cakes? Use one or two words for the answer.
   Fat insufficiently rubbed in:

....

Too much fat:

....

Too much liquid:

....

Oven too cool:

....

Fruit wet:

....

Too little liquid:

....

Too much baking powder:

....

Oven too hot:

....

Fat to flour ratio incorrect:

....

46 Name two different types of oven suitable for baking.

....

47 List the quality points you would look for in baked goods.

....

....

....

48 State any problems you have observed recently when producing any baked products. List how you will overcome these problems.

....

....

....

....

....

....

....

....

49 List some common faults found in sponges.
Example Close texture, caused by underbeating of eggs; too much flour; oven too cool or too hot.

....

....

....

....

50 The following are common faults to be found in the production of genoese. State why they could occur.

Close texture:

....

....

....

....

Sunken:

....

....

....

....

Heavy:

....

....

....

....

51 Using a basic 24 cm (10 in) genoese sponge, create a filling and finish which should be suitable for a special occasion. Give a suitable occasion and design the top accordingly.

52 List six afternoon tea pastries which use a sponge or cake mixing.

....

....

....

53 List any trends you have observed in the production of cakes and sponges.
Example Information on different types of ingredients, pre-mixes, etc.

....

....

....

....

54 In today's pastry units, sponges are more and more used in sheet form (40 × 60 cm) or in round 1–2 cm high discs. List the ingredients required to make an almond type sponge sheet, biscuit jaconde, biscuit viennoise or almond roulade and describe the method of production, baking and storing the sheets.

55 Explain the production process when making a mix for 'Othello' buns or 'biscuit à la cuillère' (split mix).

....

....

....

....

....

56 Explain why sheet sponges, e.g. roulades/Swiss rolls, are baked at 225–250°C for 4–7 minutes.

....

....

Describe the type of texture obtained (on the paper side) if a sheet of roulade is baked on silicone paper in place of greaseproof.

....

....

57 Dobos (Tobosche) sponge/biscuits mix is a Hungarian speciality from which the famous 'Dobos torte' is made.

   a Explain the method for making the mix, sheeting, baking and cutting the bases.

   ....

   ....

   ....

   ....

   ....

   ....

   b Describe briefly the texture and eating quality of the baked sheets/biscuits.

   ....

   ....

   ....

58 GMS is the main ingredient for all commercial sponge emulsifier.

   a State what GMS stands for.

   ....

   b List all ingredients required to make a sponge mix using a sponge emulsifier.

   ....

   ....

   ....

   ....

   ....

   ....

c Write out the method, in easy to follow stages, for making the sponges, including baking temperature and times.

....

....

....

....

....

....

....

....

....

59 Present three product sketches, using different sponge sheets and fillings, and give a brief indication as to the composition for three different afternoon tea pastries (pâtisserie française), assembled in a frame or moulds or as slices. Use a separate piece of paper for your sketches (see blank pages at the end of the workbook).

Unit 3NF5

Prepare, process and finish complex pastillage, marzipan, chocolate and sugar products

3NF5.1 *Prepare, process and finish complex pastillage, marzipan products and decorative icings*

Read *Advanced Practical Cookery* pages 529–31.

1   List two recipes for pastillage, one using gum tragacanth, the other using gelatine.

....

....

....

....

....

....

2   Why is cornflour used as an ingredient in pastillage?

....

....

3   Suggest an alternative starch to cornflour.

....

4   How should colour be added to pastillage?

....

....

5   List the specialised equipment you require when working with pastillage.

....

....

....

6   Describe how pastillage should be:
    Rolled:

....

....

    Cut:

....

....

7   How does the texture of pastillage affect the overall working quality and performance?

....

....

8   How is pastillage assembled?

....

....

9   Pastillage after making should be allowed to rest for 24 hours, completely covered with polythyene or clingfilm in an airtight container to prevent drying out. What are the problems associated with pastillage if used immediately?

....

....

10 Why are the following working principles essential when using pastillage?
    a The table is spotlessly clean.

....

....

b The environment is clean.

....

....

c The atmosphere is dry.

....

....

11 The cut pieces of pastillage must be allowed to dry, turning during the drying process. What may the pieces be allowed to dry on?

a Glass

b ....

c ....

d ....

12 Why is the use of food templates so important when working with pastillage?

....

....

13 Suggest an alternative gum to tragacanth that may be used in the production of pastillage.

....

....

14 If during working the pastillage starts to toughen and dry out, how can this be rectified?

....

....

15 Design a display centrepiece to follow a theme of your choice using pastillage. Name the theme and sketch the centrepiece using colour. Describe all the stages needed to make and finish the centrepiece. Finally, describe how you would present and display the finished piece to achieve maximum effect.

16   Give a brief description of the product fondant.

....

....

17   At what temperature should fondant be used?

....

18   As fondant rises in temperature, the sugar crystal gets larger and thus less light can pass through. What effect does this have on the finished product?

....

19   When thinning fondant, it is advisable to use a syrup solution. What is the degree Baumé for the syrup?

....

20   Why add glycerine to royal icing? What effect does the addition of acetic acid have?

....

....

21   Name two ways in which the air may be dispersed from royal icing apart from mixing under vacuum.

....

....

22   What is the name of the machine that mixes under vacuum?

....

23   Name a commercial product suitable for covering sponges and rich fruit cakes to give a decorative finish that may be piped over.

....

24 List the specialised tools now available for enhancing the decorative appearance of soft-moulded icings. Enhance your answer with drawings.

25 American frosting is another type of decorative icing. Name two others.

....

26 What hygiene precautions must be taken into account during the production of boiled buttercream?

....

....

....

27 When finishing a rich fruit cake with royal icing, describe by the use of drawings six decorative edges that may be used. State what number tubes and shapes you would employ.

28 What texture should royal icing be for run-outs?

....

29 Good quality wax paper is ideal when making royal icing run-outs. If wax paper is unavailable, what could you use?

....

30 Using your creativity and imagination, design a three-tier wedding cake, stating the sizes of each tier. Make maximum use of labelling to describe the design.

31 What special care must be taken when producing run-outs?

a ....

b ....

c ....

d ....

e ....

32 What are the appropriate drying conditions for run-outs and how should they be stored?

....

....

33 Name the two distinct types of almond used in marzipan.

....

34 How is marzipan made commercially?

....

....

....

35 Hard granulated sugar and white of egg is added to the almond paste to produce commercial ....

36 List six products using marzipan.
Example Battenburg

....

....

....

37 What gum solution is used to finish English rout biscuits?

....

38 Describe the production of six marzipan petit fours. Sketch the finishes and any variation in the space provided.

39 List four hygiene principles that have to be taken into account when working with marzipan.

....

....

....

....

40 List any special equipment you would use for specialised marzipan products.

....

....

41 How should marzipan goods be stored?

....

....

42 Describe briefly how you would cover a rich fruit cake with marzipan.

....

....

43 Using the circle, design a marzipan plaque with two marzipan flowers and leaves with an inscription of your choice.

44 *Macaroon recipe*

200 g (8 oz) icing sugar
4 egg whites
vanilla essence
25 g (1 oz) caster sugar for the meringue

What weight of ground almonds is required to make the above recipe workable?

....

45 Describe briefly the making of three different, quick, cut out marzipan flowers and present sketches of the finished flowers and the cutters used (use the blank pages at the end of this workbook).

e.g.

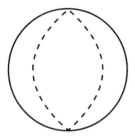  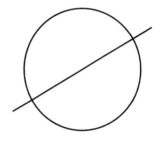

46 Describe the process and components needed to make a commercially viable, small table presentation piece, presented on a 20 cm (8") cake board, to be made from one or a combination of the following materials – pastillage, marzipan, cover paste, royal icing, runouts. Present a colour sketch of the finished presentation piece.

3NF5.2 *Prepare, process and finish complex chocolate coatings and couverture-based products*

Read *Advanced Practical Cookery* pages 531–8.

1 Why should chocolate be treated with great care?

....

....

2 List six items of equipment needed when working with chocolate, and any additional equipment you like to use.

   a Thermometer

   b Double ....

   c Dipping ....

   d ....

   e ....

   f ....

3 Why is cooking chocolate unsuitable for moulding?

....

....

4 How does cooking chocolate or chocolate substitute differ from couverture?

....

....

5 Real chocolate is produced from cocoa beans, roasted and ground to produce a

   ....

6 Cocoa butter and chocolate liquor forms the basis of all chocolate products; the higher the percentage of cocoa solids contained in the chocolate, the

   .... the chocolate.

7 How should chocolate be melted?

....

8 The temperature should not go above ....°C (..........°F).

9 Workable consistency of chocolate is around 40 to ....°C (104 to ....°F).

10 How should chocolate be heated in a microwave?

....

....

11 Why is tempering necessary?

....

....

12 When tempering, the chocolate is first allowed to reach ....°C (..........°F), and then cooled to 25 to 27°C (.......... to ....°F). The temperature is then raised to 31 to 32°C (.......... to ....°F).

13 List three points to remember when tempering chocolate.
    a Do not attempt to melt chocolate over direct heat.

    b ....

    c ....

14 Name three ingredients that may be added to chocolate.

....

....

15 Describe the making of piping ganache used for decorating and name the ingredients used.

....

....

....

....

16 Give a recipe for hand moulding chocolate.

....

....

17 Many different moulds are now available for use in making confectionery. List the moulds you have recently used and explain what special care has to be taken with the moulds.

....

....

....

18 How should finished chocolate goods be protected?

....

....

19 Outline the procedure for dipping chocolates.

....

....

....

20 Give a recipe for white chocolate truffles. List any variations you are familiar with.

....

....

....

21 Using your imagination and creative flair, design ten finishes for individual chocolates or chocolate pastries.

22 Describe the process of chocolate marbling, using a combination of white and dark chocolate.

....

....

23 When would you use a spray gun on chocolate pieces?

....

24 Packaging chocolates is highly sophisticated for preservation and for psychological reasons. Suggest suitable packaging for chocolates that will both preserve the product and enhance the appearance.

....

....

25 Describe the method and state clearly in °C, the temperatures of the ingredients when making a chocolate mousse using only milk, chocolate couverture and whipping cream.

....

....

....

....

....

....

26 List the composition of chocolate flavoured compound (bakers chocolate) and state the suitable temperature range for melting and working with the said compound.

....

....

27 List the cost price for 1 kg of

    a chocolate flavoured compound ....

    b plain couverture, 42–50% cocoa solids ....

    c white chocolate couverture ....

28 Explain why all chocolate and compounds should not be heated above 50–55°C.

....

    ᵇ State the percentage of oil that can be added to chocolate flavoured compound (bakers chocolate) and explain what effect this will have on finished coated products.

....

....

29 Explain why couverture chocolate should not be mixed with chocolate flavoured compound (bakers chocolate).

....

Explain why chocolate flavoured compound cannot be classed as chocolate.

....

3NF5.3 *Process and finish complex sugar-based products*

Read *Advanced Practical Cookery* pages 522–29.

1 Sugar is one of the most complicated foods used in food production. It can also be one of the most dangerous. Why?

....

....

2 Sugar is known to be hygroscopic. What does this mean?

....

3 What effect does this have on the handling properties?

....

....

4 State the hygiene precautions to be followed when working with sugar.

....

....

....

....

5 The amount of glucose you add to the sugar and water will vary depending on the effect you wish to achieve. Describe briefly the effects on the finished product if too much glucose has been added to a sugar solution for pulled sugar.

....

....

6 Name an ingredient which could be added to a sugar solution if glucose is unavailable, to obtain a similar type of solution.

....

7 List two non-crystalline sugars.

....

8 What kind of a sugar is honey?

....

9 How should colour be added to boiled sugar?

....

10 What advantages does powder colour have over liquid colour, if any?

....

....

11 List the specialised equipment you are aware of which is used when working with pulled, blown and poured sugar.

....

....

....

12 What are the reasons for using a gas jet?

....

....

13 One reason for adding calcium carbonate to poured sugar is to give an opaque effect. Give another reason.

....

....

14 State the percentage of calcium carbonate required and the temperature at which it is to be added.

....

15 How should completed sugar work be kept?

....

16 Design a centrepiece using poured sugar. The design should suggest a modern theme and be relatively quick and easy to produce.

17 For what purpose are the following used:
    Template:

    ....

    Plasticine:

    ....

    Spray gun:

    ....

    Copper boiler:

    ....

    Marble slab:

    ....

    Paper cone:

    ....

18 State the method for, and two uses of, spun sugar.

    ....

    ....

    ....

19 *Rock sugar recipe*
    500 g (1 lb) sugar cubes
    200 mls (⅜ pt) water

    How much royal icing is required?

    ....

20 Give two uses of rock sugar.

    ....

21 What is blown sugar used for?

....

22 Why is it advisable to use an infra-red lamp when working with blown sugar?

....

....

23 What is meant by the word 'sanitised' when applied to sugar cooking?

....

....

24 Describe the process of pulling sugar.

....

....

....

....

25 Why would you use a heat gun?

....

....

26 Why might fruits weep after being dipped in boiling sugar?

....

....

27 Describe in simple terms the chemical change which takes place when boiling sugar.

....

....

28 Describe the method of making caramel.

....

....

....

29 Complete the following sugar table:

Stage of sugar boiling	Description	Uses	Temperature
Small thread		Stock syrup	104°C . . . °F
Large thread	Threads are more numerous and stronger		110°C . . . °F
Soft ball	Sugar forms a soft ball	Fondant	116°C . . . °F
Hard ball		Sweets Petits fours	121°C . . . °F
Small crack		Meringue	. . . °C . . . °F
Large crack		Dipping fruits	153°C . . . °F
Caramel			. . . °C . . . °F

For many pastry dishes, such as ice-cream and sorbets, sugar syrups of a definite density are required.

30 What is meant by density?

....

....

31 How is density measured?

....

....

32 What is a saccharometer?

....

....

33 At what density should the syrup be for sorbet? (Give your answer in degrees Baumé.)

....

34 Why is this knowledge of syrup density important for the pastry department?

....

....

35 State why the density of syrup has to be correct when poaching different types of fruit.

....

....

36 How does the density of syrup differ with the ripeness of the fruit?

....

....

37   Complete the following table.

Sugar dissolved in 250 ml (1 pt) water		Reading on Baumé saccharometer at 30°C (60°F)
g	oz	
50	2	5°
100	4	. . . .
150	6	12°
200	8	15°
250	10	18°
300	12	. . . .
350	14	23°
400	16	24.5°
450	18	. . . .
500	20	28°
550	22	. . . .
600	24	30°

38   Explain the method you would use:

   a in making a DIRECT caramel ....

   ....

   b to obtain a fine, strong caramel taste...

   ....

39   Describe how you would use the following sugar syrup solutions in two different products from each syrup:

   a Syrup at 18°B ....

   ....

b Syrup at 22°B...

....

c Syrup at 28–30°B ....

....

40 a If you mix warm water and a high percentage of caster sugar and leave it for 24 hours to stand, what °Baume will the resulting syrup register?

....

b Explain why you should use a syrup of 22°B in preference to water to thin down fondant.

....

41 Explain how to utilise overcooked, dark caramel sugar in making coffee extract.

....

42 Describe the process used in piping out and assembling a 'sugar fountain' and present a sketch of the designs you would use. You may use a separate page for the sketches (see blank pages at the end of the book).

....

....

....

....

43 Explain and list the method, in easy to follow stages, for the making of hazelnut or almond 'praline/krokant' for the use of flavouring creams/fillings.

....

....

....

....

44 Explain the method of production you would employ when making a selection of four types of 'marzipan/fruits deguisées' (100 of each). The answer should include reference to preparation of fruits, nuts, marzipan, shaping etc. and the finishing in cooked sugar.

....

....

....

....

....

....

....

....

....

Record of Achievement – Completion of Unit 3NF5

Candidate's signature ....

Assessor's signature ....

Date ....

Notes

Notes

Notes

Notes

Notes